THE CHOCOLATE TOUCH

by
Patrick Skene Catling

Teacher Guide

Written by
Anne Troy
Joan Primeaux

Note

The Bantam Skylark paperback edition of the book was used to prepare this guide. The page references may differ in the hardcover or other paperback editions.

Please note: Please assess the appropriateness of this book for the age level and maturity of your students prior to reading and discussing it with your class.

ISBN 1-56137-047-9

Copyright infringement is a violation of Federal Law.

© 2000, 2004 by Novel Units, Inc., Bulverde, Texas. All rights reserved. No part of this publication may be reproduced, translated, stored in a retrieval system, or transmitted in any way or by any means (electronic, mechanical, photocopying, recording, or otherwise) without prior written permission from Novel Units, Inc.

Photocopying of student worksheets by a classroom teacher at a non-profit school who has purchased this publication for his/her own class is permissible. Reproduction of any part of this publication for an entire school or for a school system, by for-profit institutions and tutoring centers, or for commercial sale is strictly prohibited.

Novel Units is a registered trademark of Novel Units, Inc.

Printed in the United States of America.

To order, contact your local school
supply store, or—

Novel Units, Inc.
P.O. Box 433
Bulverde, TX 78163-0433

Web site: www.educyberstor.com

Table of Contents

Skills and Strategies

Thinking
  Brainstorming

Writing
  Narrative, creative

Listening/Speaking
  Discussion, drama, role play

Comprehension
  Predicting, cause and effect,
  sequencing

Literary Elements
  Characterization, story
  elements

Summary

John found an old coin with his initials on it. This was the beginning of a strange adventure with his favorite kind of food—chocolate candy. Or is candy food?

Initiating Activity

1. Place on each child's desk a small piece of chocolate wrapped in foil—perhaps candy kisses. Ask children what this could be? Brainstorm the word **chocolate**.

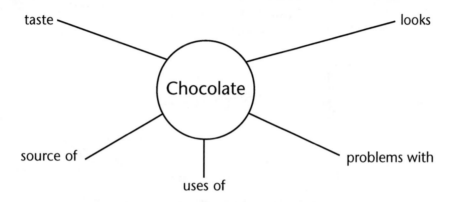

2. Distribute books. What is unusual about the illustration? (*Boy is kissing his mother. Her face looks funny—she's turning to chocolate.*)

   The Chocolate Touch is like another story we have read. It was *King Midas and the Golden Touch*. (There are many different editions. It is available in Scholastic Paperback.) The King Midas story may be read to the children.

Recommended Procedure

This book will be read one section at a time using DRTA (Directed Reading Thinking Activity) Method. This technique involves reading a section, predicting what will happen next (making good guesses) based on what has already occurred in the story. The children continue to read and verify predictions at the end of each chapter.

Using Predictions

We all make predictions as we read—little guesses about what will happen next, how the conflict will be resolved, which details given by the author will be important to the plot, which details will help to fill in our sense of a character. Students should be encouraged to predict, to make sensible guesses. As students work on predictions, these discussion questions can be used to guide them: What are some of the ways to predict? What is the process of a sophisticated reader's thinking and predicting? What clues does an author give us to help us in making our predictions? Why are some predictions more likely than others?

A predicting chart is for students to record their predictions. As each subsequent chapter is discussed, you can review and correct previous predictions. This procedure serves to focus on predictions and to review the stories.

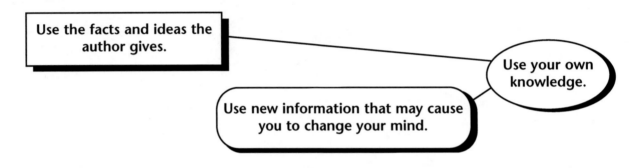

Prediction Chart

What characters have we met so far?	What is the conflict in the story?	What are your predictions?	Why did you make those predictions?

Using Attribute Webs

Attribute Webs are simply a visual representation of a character from the novel. They provide a systematic way for the students to organize and recap the information they have about a particular character. Attribute webs may be used after reading the novel to recapitulate information about a particular character or completed gradually as information unfolds, done individually, or finished as a group project.

One type of character attribute web uses these divisions:
- How a character acts and feels. (How does the character feel in this picture? How would you feel if this happened to you? How do you think the character feels?)
- How a character looks. (Close your eyes and picture the character. Describe him to me.)
- Where a character lives. (Where and when does the character live?)
- How others feel about the character. (How does another specific character feel about our character?)

In group discussion about the student attribute webs and specific characters, the teacher can ask for backup proof from the novel. You can also include inferential thinking.

Attribute webs need not be confined to characters. They may also be used to organize information about a word, concept, object or place. See the examples on the following pages.

Attribute Webs

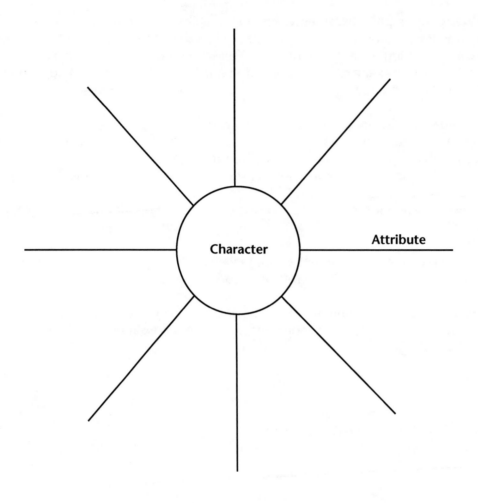

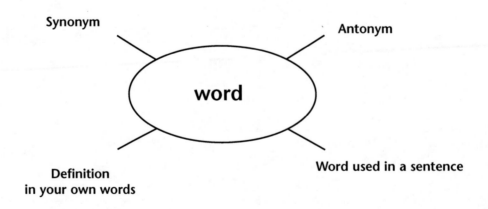

© Novel Units, Inc.

6

Character Attribute Web

The attribute web below is designed to help you gather clues the author provides about what a character is like. Fill in the blanks with words and phrases which tell how the character acts and looks, as well as what the character says and what others say about him or her.

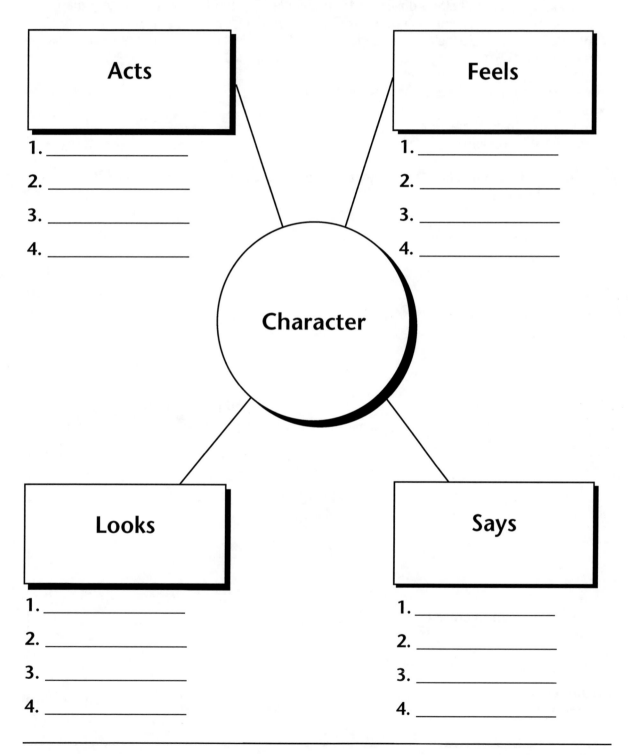

Story Maps

Many stories have the same parts—a setting, characters, a problem, a goal, and a series of events that lead to an ending or conclusion. These story elements may be placed on a story map. Just as a road map helps a driver get from one place to another, so, too, a story map leads a reader from one point to another. There are many different types of story maps; two are included in this guide (below, and pages 9 and 19). Students may use the types included or make up their own.

What information do we have to begin a story map?
- What is the setting?
- Who is the main character?
- What is the problem?

As the story is read more characters may be added, the setting and problem (especially in this story) may change.

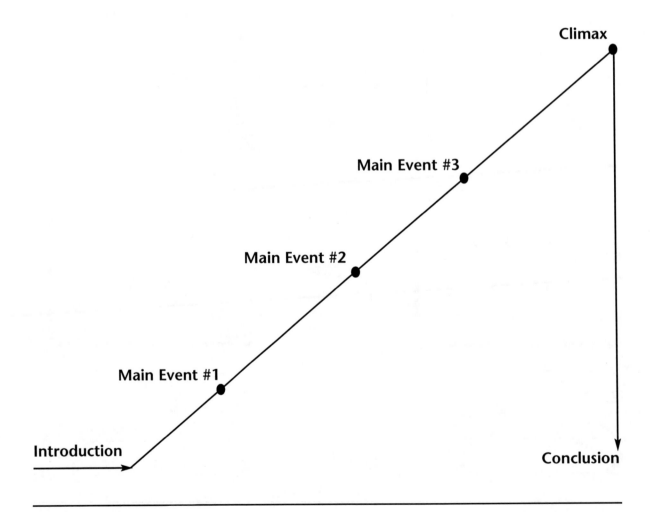

Story Map

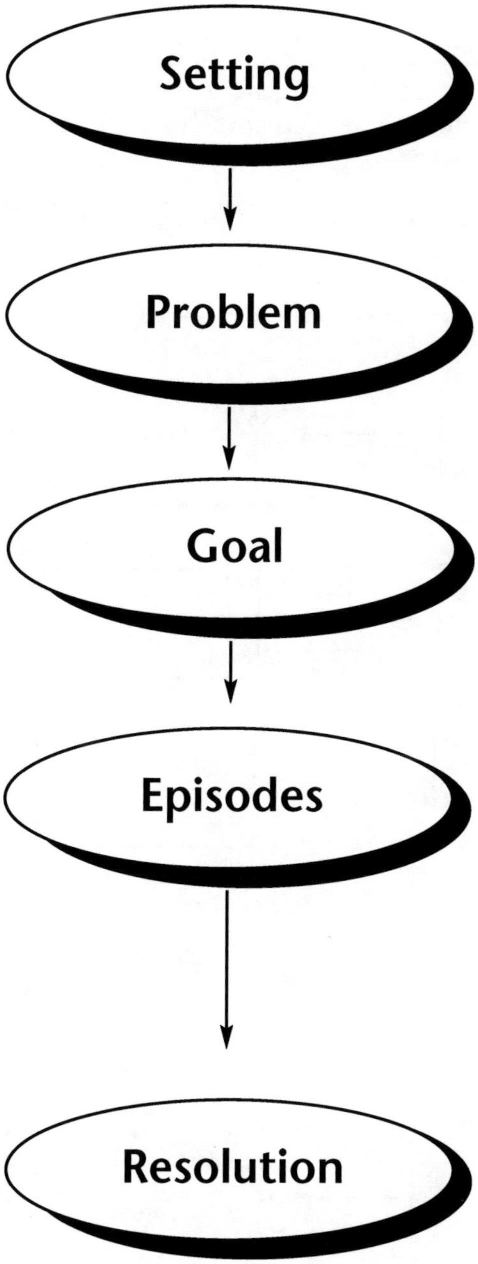

Characters_____

_____

_____

_____

Setting

↓

Problem

Time and Place_____

_____

_____

Goal

_____

_____

↓

Beginning ⟶ Development ⟶ Outcome

Episodes

_____

_____

_____

_____

↓

_____

Resolution

_____

_____

_____

_____

Cause-Effect Map

Directions

When examining the reasons for events in a story, we often find that one cause has several results, or that several causes lead to the same result.

To plot cause and effect in a story, first list the sequence of events. Then mark causes with a C and effects with an E. Use an arrow from the cause to the effect. Remember that many effects cause something else so they might be marked with an E and a C with an arrow to the next effect.

1. Think about the various effects of the main events in *The Chocolate Touch*. Organize the chain of events it sets off within the map below.

2. Organize some of these reasons (causes of actions) within the second map below.

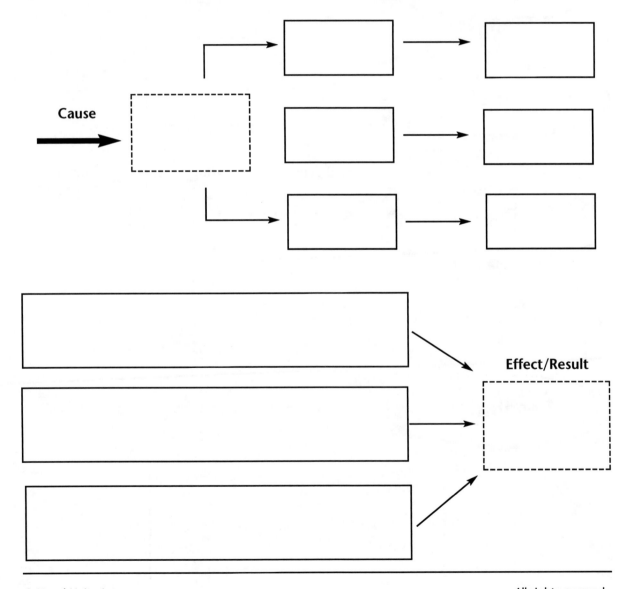

Chapter-by-Chapter

Vocabulary, Discussion Questions, and Activities

Chapter 1   Pages 1-9

Vocabulary
brigands 2	devoured 4	gravely 4	anxiously 5
reproved 7	complications 7	shrugged 8	persisted 9
emphatically 9			

Discussion Questions
1. What was John's one fault? (*p. 2, He was a pig about candy.*) Do you think that is very bad? Why or why not? How many of you share John's fault?

2. What was the doctor's advice to John? (*p. 7, less candy*)

3. Have your parents ever talked about a balanced diet like John's did? Have you studied the food groups in health? Role play: Mr. or Mrs. Midas talking to John or your parents talking to you.

4. Why do you think John's bad habit with candy made his mother unhappy? (*p. 9, She knew that what the doctor said about all sorts of complications was serious. She worried about John.*)

5. Do you think John understands what his father is saying on page 9? Why or why not?

Prediction
Will John change? What could make him change?

Story Map Activity
Have your students complete a story map like the ones on pages 8 and 9 of this guide, or have them make up their own. Near the end of the novel, have them complete another story map and compare the two.

Writing Activity
There are no chapter titles in this book. After your students have read a chapter, have them write a title that would make the reader want to read it. Have each compare his/her title with a classmate's.

Vocabulary

absentmindedly 10	absolutely 12	beckoning 12	heartily 12
ingredients 12	heavily laden 14	cellophane 15	declined 15
coaxing 17	encountered 19		

Discussion Questions

1. Describe the coin John found. Illustrate it.

2. What was John going to do with the coin? (*p. 11, He was going to show it to Susan.*)

3. What is mysterious about the storekeeper? (*p. 12, Store open on Sunday. Man knew John's name. p. 14 The man will only accept John's kind of money.*)

4. How was John dishonest? (*p. 15, He said his mother would let him buy the big box of chocolates. pp. 15-16 He crept into the house with the chocolate box. Hid the box of chocolate under his bed. Didn't tell his parents why he didn't go to Susan's house. Pretended to be sleepy so he could go to bed early.*)

Prediction
Why do you think there was only one chocolate in the box?

Activity
Begin an attribute web for John. (See Using Attribute Webs, page 5.)

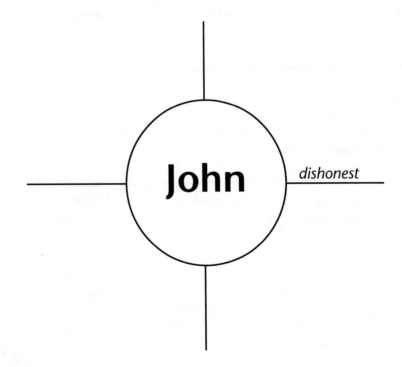

Vocabulary
ambled 21

Discussion Questions
1. Do you think the toothpaste would be chocolate if Mary tried it? (*p. 23*)

2. If you were John's mother, would you have suspected something when John ate his breakfast? Why or why not?

3. Why was John's mother puzzled? (*p. 26, He said he didn't need a dime to buy chocolate.*)

4. How do you know this book was published some time ago? *(One cannot buy any chocolate candy for a dime.)* Prove it. *(Introduce students to copyright date in the front of the book.)*

Prediction
What will happen to John at school?

Writing Activity
If you were John, what would you do with your chocolate touch? What would you like to turn into chocolate? What would you tell your parents, sisters and brothers, and friends?

Vocabulary

marmalade 28	devouring 29	sneered 29	slyest 29
contentedly 30	resist 30	snatched 30	soggy 32
triumphs 33	suspiciously 33	reluctantly 33	crescent 34
embarrassment 34			

Discussion Questions

1. Why did John let Spider have the glove? (*p. 30, Spider was older, the meanest and slyest boy. John had enough chocolate.*)

2. Why was Spider disgusted and disappointed with John's glove? (*p. 32, It did not turn to chocolate for him.*)

3. Why did Susan react with tears telling John she hated him? (*p. 34, He turned her coin to chocolate.*)

4. What did the author compare Susan's tears to? (*p. 34, "Tears trickled down her cheeks like rain down a windowpane."*)

Prediction

What will happen to John? Will he enjoy his chocolate touch or will he have more problems? What kind of problems?

Vocabulary Activity

Have students use the vocabulary words from the chapter (and past chapters) to make crossword puzzles on graph paper. The students should write questions for each word and develop an answering sheet. Have students exchange puzzles.

Chapter 5 Pages 35-41

Vocabulary

scuffling 35	surveyed 36	spectacles 36	accurately 37
corridor 37	treadle 37	reprovingly 38	apparently 39
concentrating 39	cautioned 39		

Discussion Questions

1. Do you think John is frightened by these strange happenings? Would you be frightened or how would you feel?

2. What can you add to John's attribute web?

3. Why do you think only some things that John touches turn to chocolate?

Role Play Activity

If you were Miss Plimsole what would you say to John? If you were John how would you try to explain your problem?

Chapter 6 Pages 42-47

Vocabulary

scorned 44	preferred 44	sacrifice 44	protested 45
reproachfully 45	hooted 45	retorted 47	

Discussion Questions

1. Why do you think Miss Plimsole said she was going to have a talk with the nurse about John? (p. 43) Why didn't she punish him?

2. How did the girls and Susan treat John? What do you think the girls whispered? (p. 45)

Prediction

How is he going to solve them?

Activity

Have students list John's problems. (p. 45)
- mother would be cross about the gloves
- messed-up arithmetic test
- had terrible thirst
- had sticky, dry mouth

How would they solve them if they were John?

Chapter 7 Pages 48-53

Vocabulary

throng 49	spacious 49	enviously 49	transformed 53
opaque 53	cutlery 53	utensils 53	

Discussion Questions

1. John imagines the taste of cold, creamy milk. What does John want more than anything else? *(p. 49, Something that was thirst quenching.)*

2. John had a plan to eat his lunch without anything touching his lips. Why doesn't this work? *(p. 50, The magic touch is getting worse.)*

3. Why did John choose certain foods for lunch? *(pp. 50-51, They were healthy foods. Maybe he was trying to stop the chocolate touch.)*

Prediction

John is going to the playground. Will he be able to play like the other children?

Activity

Add more words to John's attribute web. *(p. 53, horrified, frightened.)*

Chapter 8 Pages 54-61

Vocabulary

incident 54	avarice 55	indigestion 55	acidity 55
moderation 55	digestibility 55	auditorium 55	poised 57
unison 58	uproarious 61	derisively 61	

Discussion Questions

1. How were all the spelling words on page 55 related to John's problem with the chocolate touch?

2. What words describe John as he tries to play his trumpet solo? Did you guess what was going to happen?

Prediction

Will John get help?

Vocabulary Activity

Have students prepare for a vocabulary definition bee by writing definitions for each word on 3x5 index cards, to be used by the leader of the bee.

Chapter 9

Vocabulary

humiliation 62   indignant 62   lunged 66

Discussion Questions

1 Why is John angry with everyone? *(p. 62, He felt everyone had turned against him.)*

2. If you were John, would you have been afraid to go to the party? Why or why not? (p. 64)

3. How do you think Susan's guests reacted when the water turned to chocolate syrup?

4. Look at the illustration on page 67. What do you think John is thinking? Write down his thoughts. Share your ideas with a classmate.

Cooperative Group Activity

How should John solve his problem? To whom should he go? How can he make them understand? Write a plan as a group. The class will see how many ways there might be to solve a problem.

Chapter 10

Vocabulary

assured 70   protested 71   elixir 73   chocolatified 75
unprecedented 75   exhaustive 75

Discussion Questions

1. To help John, his father suggested they return to the candy store to discuss John's problem with the storekeeper. Do you think this is a good idea? Why or why not? Why didn't it work?

2. Do you think John has a problem that a doctor could solve?

3. Look at the illustration on page 74. What is John's father thinking? Write down his thoughts.

Prediction

Could this be a dream John is having? Is this a story that could happen? Why or why not? What do we call this kind of story? *(fantasy)*

Activity

Complete the Cause-Effect Map (or one like it) on page 10.

Vocabulary

untidy 78	proprietor 78	pleasantries 78	babbled 78
unselfishness 79	evident 79	acquiring 81	frantically 81

Discussion Questions

1. When did John forget himself? What really upset John? (*p. 77 When he kissed his mother and turned her to a chocolate statue.*)

2. What reason did the storekeeper give for John finding the coin? (*p. 81 "...you yourself earned the coin...Only greedy people can even see that kind of money."*)

3. What choices did the storekeeper give John? (*p. 81 "...If you had to choose between getting rid of your chocolate touch and restoring your mother to life, which would it be?"*)

4. Why is the storekeeper polishing another coin? (*p. 83 "...ready for a new set of initials in case the need for them should arise."*)

Prediction

Will John's mother be all right?

Writing Activity

Have students write a letter to John, telling him what he should or should not do, concerning his mother.

Discussion Questions
  1. Look at the illustration on page 84. What happened? *(The candy store has disappeared again.)*

  2. Does John's mother know what happened? *(p. 85)*

  3. Did John learn his lesson? Why or why not?

Story Map Activity
A story map is just a simple drawing that helps you see how the important parts of a story fit together. It also helps you remember what happened in the story when talking or writing about it. See pages 8 and 9 of this guide for more examples of story maps.

Fill in the story map.
  1. Briefly describe the setting, or time and place, in which the story begins.

  2. Describe the main problem.

  3. Summarize at least three key events in the story.

  4. Tell what the climax was. In other words, where was the point of greatest tension, where you knew the problem couldn't get any worse?

  5. Describe the resolution, or what happened after the climax until the end of the story.

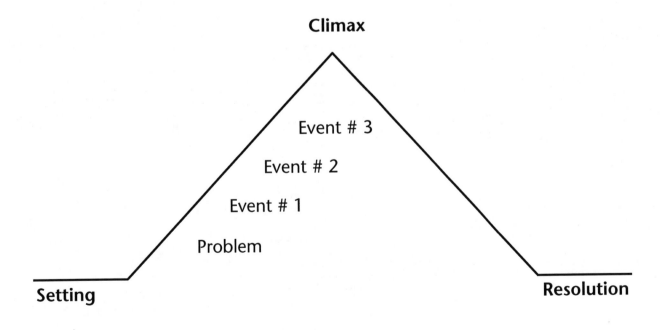

Extension Activities

Choose one and be prepared to share it with the group.

1. Drama
Think about your favorite part of the story.
Think about how it could be acted out.
Choose the actors from our reading group, practice, then perform it for the rest of the group.

2. Research
Read the last page in the book (the About the Author section). Be prepared to explain these facts about *The Chocolate Touch*:

The year it was first published.
The place the author was born.
The place the author lives now.
The quotes from the two newspapers ("The New York Herald Tribune" and "The Saturday Review") about the book.

Look in the card catalog to find other books by this author.

3. Art
Reread the description of the coin on page 11.
Use oaktag to make a magic coin for yourself.

Creative Writing

Choose one of the following topics and write about it. Then illustrate it.

1. What do you think the storekeeper in the magic candy store was trying to make John understand?

2. Tests always made John nervous. How do you feel about tests?

3. Why do you think the storekeeper is making another magic coin?

4. If you had the choice between being John Midas with the chocolate touch or King Midas with the golden touch, which would you choose and why? Make sure you include events that made you very happy and events that made you miserable. How was your problem solved? Illustrate your story.

Assessment for *The Chocolate Touch*

Assessment is an ongoing process. The following ten items can be completed during the novel study. Once finished, the student and teacher will check the work. Points may be added to indicate the level of understanding.

Name _____ Date _____

Student   **Teacher**

_____   _____   1. Keep a predicting chart as you read the book.

_____   _____   2. Explain "predicting" and "cause and effect" in short paragraphs. Use examples from the book.

_____   _____   3. Fill in a story map to review the book's plot.

_____   _____   4. Display attribute webs for the book's main characters.

_____   _____   5. Sort the vocabulary words into categories, e.g., nouns, actions, chocolate descriptions.

_____   _____   6. Design a visual aid for the book.

_____   _____   7. Make up five literal questions about the book. Use them for a *Chocolate Touch* Bee or *Chocolate Touch* Jeopardy.

_____   _____   8. Create a comic strip of the main events in the story.

_____   _____   9. Dramatize a favorite scene in the story.

_____   _____   10. Write a letter to your principal praising or panning the book.

Comments:

Notes

Notes